CONSTRUCTION WORKER

Rachel O'Connor

HIGH
interest
books

Children's Press®
A Division of Scholastic Inc.
New York / Toronto / London / Auckland / Sydney
Mexico City / New Delhi / Hong Kong
Danbury, Connecticut

Book Design: Christopher Logan and Daniel Hosek
Layout and Production: Mindy Liu
Contributing Editors: Kevin Somers and Scott Waldman
Photo Credits: Cover © Walter Hodges/Corbis; p. 4 © Index Stock Imagery, Inc.; pp. 7, 23 © Raymond Gehman/Corbis; p. 8 © Yann Arthus-Betrand/Corbis; p. 11 © Angelo Hornak/Corbis; p. 12 © Gary Buss/Getty Images; p. 15 © Annie Griffiths Belt/Corbis; p. 16 © Richard Klune/Corbis; p. 19 © Photodisc/Getty Images; p. 20 © Paris Claude/Corbis Sygma; p. 25 © John and Lisa Merrill/Corbis; p. 26 © Robert Maass/Corbis; p. 28 © Gary Kufner/Corbis; p. 31 © Patrick Bennett/Corbis; p. 33 © Vince Streano/Corbis; p. 34 © Strauss/Curtis/Corbis; p. 37 © Bettmann/Corbis; p. 39 © Bill Miles/Corbis; pp. 40–41 © Pete Saloutos/Corbis

Library of Congress Cataloging-in-Publication Data

O'Connor, Rachel.
    Construction worker / by Rachel O'Connor.
    p. cm.—(Great jobs)
    Summary: Discusses some of the jobs done by construction workers, the training and tools needed, and opportunities in the field.
    Includes bibliographical references and index.
    ISBN 0-516-24089-7 (lib. bdg.)—ISBN 0-516-25923-7 (pbk.)
    1. Building—Vocational guidance—Juvenile literature. 2. Construction workers—Juvenile literature. [1. Building trades—Vocational guidance. 2. Construction workers. 3. Vocational guidance.] I. Title. II. Series.

TH149.O28 2003
690'.023—dc22

                                        2003012311

Contents

It's the day after a huge storm has passed through your town. You and your construction crew drive up to a house. You're amazed to see the damage caused during the night by the storm's high winds and heavy rain. A large tree has fallen through the roof and crashed into the living room. Rainwater has ruined the furniture and rugs. Thankfully, no one had been sleeping there at the time. The family is standing in front of the house when you arrive. They still have their pajamas on. They spent the night in a motel, but it looks like none of them have gotten any sleep. They look tired and upset by the damage done to their home.

The trunk of the tree had caved in part of the roof. A few of the larger tree branches tore through the couch, hit the television, and broke apart the wall between the kitchen and dining room. You and your fellow construction workers walk around the

This home in Nashville, Tennessee, will need major reconstruction work to repair the damage caused by a tornado.

house, inspecting the damage. It looks pretty bad, but at least the frame of the house is not damaged. After several days of your hard work, the family could be living in their own home again.

Without wasting any time your construction crew gets to work. First, the tree is removed from the house and cut up. All the branches are then removed from the home. The roof is the first thing your crew fixes.

The damaged part is removed and rebuilt. Your crew then begins work inside the house. The workers build a new wall and replace some damaged flooring. Everyone works overtime for four straight days. By the fifth day, the repair work is finished and the family moves back in. You've completed another fine job.

The houses and buildings that we spend time in every day have one thing in common—they were all built by construction workers. Many of the houses were also repaired and renovated by construction workers. In this book, we'll learn about the construction workers who build the structures of our world.

Roofers begin repairs on a house in Homestead, Florida, after it was hit by Hurricane Andrew in 1992.

CHAPTER ONE

The People Who Make It Happen

People have been constructing houses since at least 12,000 B.C. At that time, people moved from place to place in search of food. They built houses made of stone, wood, and animal skins. After humans learned how to grow their own food, their needs changed. Houses no longer needed to be built quickly and more complicated houses could be constructed. These early houses were made of packed clay and wood.

About 10,000 years later, humans built the great pyramids in Egypt. This was an amazing construction accomplishment. The ancient Egyptians only used levers and wooden sledges to move stone blocks that weighed up to 2.5 tons (2.27 metric tons). The blocks were also stacked on top of each other, to heights of up to 481 feet (147 meters).

The Giza, Kheops, Khepren, and Mykerinos pyramids were built between 2625 and 2500 B.C. Many of the Egyptians' building techniques remain unknown, even to this day.

Romans developed many new building methods a few centuries after the Egyptians built their pyramids. The new methods allowed Roman buildings to have large roofs, arches, and domes. Many of the ancient Roman construction methods are frequently used today. Roman construction workers did such a fine job with their buildings that many of them are still standing.

Methods of construction soon reached a level which allowed humans to build today's modern skyscrapers. Buildings have gotten taller as construction workers have gotten better at their jobs. The sky is the limit for construction workers, as they build the structures of tomorrow.

Who's Who on the Construction Site

It takes many people to turn an idea into an actual structure. The person who oversees a building project is the general contractor. The general contractor hires a project manager to run the construction job and to coordinate the many activities on the construction site. The project manager tells the

The Pisa Baptistery, located in Pisa, Italy, was built over a period of about 200 years. The first three levels are an excellent example of Roman building design.

workers what the contractor wants and makes sure that these orders are carried out. He is the leader of the job. The foreman is the person who usually chooses the labor force. When they are hiring workers, foremen often consider a person's character. They want their workers to get along and work well together. An administration staff is also hired on a big project. The staff manages the building drawings, plans, and schedules. Whatever the job may be, one of the key elements of the construction process is the ability of all the different workers to cooperate with each other.

There are many different types of workers on a construction site. They range from construction laborers to many types of skilled craftworkers. First, let's take a look at construction laborers.

Construction Laborers

The work that construction laborers do is usually very physically demanding. Workers need to build their strength and stamina so that they can do heavy physical work. They have to be able to shovel and lift heavy weights. Their jobs include mixing, pouring, and leveling concrete. Laborers also dig trenches and carry loads to different areas of the site. They can help other workers on the site, such as carpenters or plasterers. Laborers also may have to load and unload materials from trucks as well as measure and mark the areas where the structure is to be built.

Members of the administration staff work closely with construction workers to make sure that building plans are followed.

This stonemason is restoring stonework on the roof of the National Cathedral in Washington, D.C.

Construction laborers take their orders from the site's foreman. However, each worker is responsible for performing his or her task well. Construction workers usually start off as helpers at the construction site. In the industry, they are known as gofers. With hard work, some construction workers advance to become construction supervisors or foremen.

Construction Craftworkers

Construction craftworkers can be divided into three categories: structural workers, finishing workers, and mechanical workers. Structural workers include brickmasons, carpenters, and operating engineers, who operate machinery. Finishing workers include roofers, drywall workers, plasterers, and painters. Mechanical workers include electricians and plumbers.

The brickmasons or stonemasons on the construction site are often referred to as bricklayers. These workers often work outdoors. They build and repair walls, floors, and other partitions. Their job includes lifting heavy bricks and working on scaffolds, which can be quite dangerous.

Bricklayers build walls from a set of drawings, on which each stone or block has been numbered. Helpers on the site usually bring these blocks to the bricklayers to be placed. Bricklayers often have to stand or kneel for long periods of time while they are working. Construction workers who do roofing, masonry, and stonework are most at risk for injuring themselves.

Carpenters work on a range of projects, from buildings to highways. They cut, fit, and put together wood and other materials. They often install doors and windows, cabinets, paneling, and maintain highways.

Today, the work of a carpenter has been made easier by the introduction of premade walls and stairs that can be lifted into place. Carpenters make up the largest group of building craftworkers. Their work involves a lot of math and mechanics.

A finishing worker has one of the dirtiest and most physically demanding jobs on a construction site. A roofer's job is to install or repair roofs. Roofs can be made of a variety of materials including tar, asphalt and gravel, or shingles made of slate, tile, or wood. Working on a roof is dangerous and roofers must always be careful as they go about their work. Drywall workers are responsible for hanging drywall on the inside walls of a house. Drywall, also called Sheetrock™, is a thin layer of plaster sandwiched between two sheets of heavy paper. Drywall is very heavy and must be handled carefully.

After the structural workers construct a building, the mechanical workers take over. Electricians run wires inside the entire building. They drill holes in the walls and floors for their wires. They hook up

Most carpenters are trained to work with a variety of materials and tools. It is common for a carpenter to be involved in a project from start to finish.

As well as installing water pipes for kitchens and bathrooms, plumbers also install piping systems which carry gas, steam, and in some cases, oil.

lighting fixtures and power outlets in the walls. Since they are working with electricity, electricians need a lot of training in their craft before they are allowed to work independently on a job.

Plumbers place pipes throughout the building. They then connect the toilets, showers, and sinks to the pipes that bring water in and out of buildings. They work with tools that cut and connect metal and plastic pipes together.

These are just some of the many types of workers involved in construction. Each worker is responsible for his or her contribution to the complete structure. Many of the construction trades are dependent on one another. This means that workers need to be able to get their work done on time so that other tradespeople can continue to work. For example, an electrician must install wires on time so that a drywall finisher can put the finishing touches on the wall.

TAKING CARE OF BUSINESS

More than $100 billion is spent on building projects each year in the United States!

CHAPTER TWO

The Construction Site

Training

There are many different types of training for construction workers. The amount of training you will need depends on the particular job you would like to do in the construction field. Some people, such as laborers, get their start in the construction industry by doing the jobs that don't require a lot of experience. They will then work their way into a skilled craftworker position by learning as they work. Others apprentice, or train, with more experienced construction workers until they are ready to work on their own.

There are many apprenticeship programs which offer on-the-job training, as well as classroom instruction. The number of hours you work will

In addition to apprenticeship programs and on-the-job training, trade schools can be a great way to learn the skills needed to be a craftworker.

Equipment such as bucket loaders are a great help to construction workers when they need to clear debris from a site.

depend on what trade you are learning. For example, an apprentice bricklayer or stonemason is usually required to do three years of on-the-job training and a minimum of 144 hours working in the classroom. Apprenticeships can last from three to five years. You need to be at least seventeen or eighteen years old to take part in many of these programs. Most building trades require you to have a high school education. Mathematical skills are useful for many fields in the construction industry.

Apprentices in these training programs are closely supervised on the construction site. The foreman and the craftworker usually tell the apprentice what he or she needs to do. Apprentices start out by doing the unskilled, physical tasks on the construction site. Their responsibilities may include cleaning up debris, operating simple machinery, or putting up and taking apart scaffolding. They work alongside experienced craftworkers to learn the basics of a trade or craft. A brickmason's helper will often only get to mix mortar. He or she will, however, be able to observe the brickmason applying the mortar, placing the brick, and joining the brick and mortar.

Machinery, Tools, and Materials

Advances in technology have greatly helped the construction industry. Workers no longer rely on their strength alone. They now have machines to help them. Cranes can lift heavy materials, such as bricks, cement, or equipment. Bulldozers and front loaders move huge loads of earth. There are even machines to pour concrete.

Construction workers usually own and look after their personal tools. Some of these tools include special hammers and chisels that masons use to cut stone. Laborers pull concrete with a hoe when they are pouring a floor. Tools must always be handled with care.

Most buildings are built with walls made of wood, steel, concrete block, stone, granite, or marble. Wood, which is strong, durable, and light, is used for decks, ladders, and scaffolding. Modern homes are usually made from wood. Steel is another material found in buildings. It is fire-resistant and very strong. Steel is used to help support buildings and other structures such as bridges. Concrete is a mixture of sand, stone, and cement which is often used for foundations.

TAKING CARE OF BUSINESS

Some of the earliest tall buildings were towers such as the San Gimignano towers in Italy. The walls of these towers were made of thick, heavy stone. There were hardly any windows because they weakened the structure.

The construction of the tall towers of San Gimignano dates back to the eleventh century.

Dangers on the Site

Construction work can be dangerous. This industry has one of the highest rates of accidents and deaths. Many deaths are due to falls, some to transportation accidents, and still others because of equipment errors. Many workers risk their lives while working in high places or in shafts. Carpenters and masons often work at great heights. They do this by standing on platforms and scaffolds. Some construction workers work hundreds of feet in the air, on narrow steel beams.

Bad weather can be a cause of accidents, too. A construction site can be dangerous when wet weather makes the site muddy and slippery. Workers can lose their footing, equipment can slide out of control, and visibility can be bad.

Safety on the Job

To protect themselves against things that fall, construction workers wear hard hats and protective boots. The project manager often holds meetings on the site to discuss safety issues. Some of the many dangers on a construction site include fire and collapse. There are safety regulations to protect construction workers from these dangers. All construction projects must follow these regulations. Buildings must conform to certain standards. Every city and state has building codes. Construction of walls, pipes, ceilings, roofs, and other structures must conform to standards that protect against fire, leaks, and collapse. Workers must make sure that the public is not in danger around a building under construction as well.

Working in high places can be dangerous. Safety has to be the first concern for this worker framing a new house near Las Vegas, Nevada.

CHAPTER THREE

A Day on the Job

Shawn is a construction foreman for Cooperstown General Contractors. He wakes up at 6:30 A.M. to get an early start on the day. He has just enough time for a quick shower and breakfast before he has to be at work. Today, he and his crew will be fixing an old farmhouse. On the way to work, he listens to the weather report. It's going to be over one hundred degrees. Shawn decides it is too hot to work on the front of the house. There are no trees to shade the workers from the Sun. He decides to have his crew hang the wooden siding on the back of the farmhouse where the trees will provide shade.

Once there, he meets with some of the other members of his construction crew to discuss what needs to be done that day. By 8:00 A.M., it is already hot.

A good foreman knows that talking to his crew is an important part of getting the job done right.

Hanging the siding on the old farmhouse is going to be hard work. The crew starts at the bottom of the house. Shawn will take the measurements and give them to Matt. Matt will cut the siding to the right size and then hand it to Tracey. She will organize the cut siding by size for Shawn so that it will be easier for him to hang. Shawn tells Tracey to set up the scaffolding so that he can work his way up to the top of the house without having to slow down.

At 10:30 A.M., the crew stops for a water break. Everyone is sweating. The temperature is high, but the job still needs to get done. Shawn makes sure that everyone has plenty of water to drink and that no one is suffering from the intense heat.

When Shawn reaches the top of the house and is getting ready to put on the last few pieces of siding, he notices a problem. The wall of the farmhouse is not even. This is not unusual for old structures. The foundation beneath the house settles as it gets older and this makes the wall slightly

Siding can be made of wood, but vinyl or aluminum siding are more popular. They are easier to maintain and less costly to install.

uneven. There will be a gap between the last piece of siding and the rest of the house. Rainwater could drip into the gap and ruin the wall underneath. Shawn climbs down the scaffolding to discuss the problem with Matt and Tracey. Matt suggests that they use a bigger piece of siding to cover the gap.

Tracey suggests that they slip a couple of thin pieces of wood underneath the piece of siding. This will make it even with the rest of the siding. Shawn agrees that this is a good idea. He takes the new piece and climbs back to the top of the scaffolding. The idea seems to work. Shawn notices that the wood underneath the siding is a little too thick. He thinks about how to make the wood fit better and decides to file it down. He takes the file out of his tool belt and uses it to shave a little bit off the piece of wood. He tries the piece again and it works.

When Shawn climbs down off the scaffolding, the crew takes a break for lunch. They have worked quickly that day. Since it's a Friday afternoon, Shawn tells them that they can leave a little early and spend more time with their families over the weekend. He knows that the happier he keeps his crew, the harder they will work to get the job done.

Heat can be a serious health risk to construction workers. To fight the heat, workers drink plenty of fluids and take rest breaks to help their bodies cool.

CHAPTER FOUR

Getting Into the Construction Industry

A lot of people enter the construction industry because they know someone working in it. Many people follow in the footsteps of their fathers, grandfathers, uncles, cousins, or other relatives. One way of getting into the construction industry is by becoming a union member. A union is a group of workers who come together to make sure that they are being paid and treated fairly. Unions also give their members information about news and trends in their trade. Most of the time, you need to know someone in a union before you can get in. However, it is not necessary to join a union to become a construction worker. Only about 21 percent of construction workers are members of unions.

Nonprofit groups are playing an important role in helping women enter the construction industry. Groups such as the National Association of Women in Construction (NAWIC) and Professional Women in Construction (PWC) work hard to help women succeed in this business.

Women in Construction

More men work in the construction industry than women. Women make up less than 25 percent of general construction workers. It has been difficult for women to enter this industry. They often face discrimination in hiring, training, and treatment by unions and construction employers. One way women have managed to enter the industry is with the help of the federal government. A federal law was passed that required contractors involved in public works to hire a certain percentage of female workers.

TAKING CARE OF BUSINESS

The Empire State Building in New York City holds the record for the fastest-built skyscraper. The world famous structure—102 floors tall—was completed in only one year and forty-five days!

The Empire State Building was the tallest building in the world when it was completed in 1931.

Getting Ahead

If you are willing to learn and put in the time, there are plenty of opportunities for advancement within the construction industry. For those who are very committed, there is the option of starting up your own business. The construction industry lends itself well to start-up businesses. Some people start out by running their business out of their home. Staying in the business and making it successful can sometimes be difficult. As the owner of a construction business, you must find the jobs, pay your workers, do a lot of the work yourself, get your clients to pay you, and then get more work. Although it is often difficult, many people manage to survive and thrive in their own businesses.

Contributing to Society

Every trade in construction is important. A building cannot be completed without the input of every

Craftspeople use a wide variety of tools to get the job finished. This craftswoman is cutting a wood plank with a circular saw.

trade or craft, from the laborer to the plasterer. Every worker knows that his or her contribution is important to the total process. Many construction workers enjoy a high level of job satisfaction. They can look on with pride as the structures they are building become taller and take shape.

People in the construction industry know that they are making an important contribution to society. They are building a piece of history. The structures they build will be around for a very long

time. The evidence of all their hard work will live on. If you are not afraid of hard work, the construction industry might be the place for you.

administration (ad-**min**-uh-stray-shun) the people who manage or direct an organization

apprentice (uh-**pren**-tiss) someone who learns a trade or craft by working with a skilled person

asphalt (**ass**-fawlt) a black, tarlike substance that is mixed with sand and gravel and then rolled flat to make roads

complicated (**kom**-pli-kay-tid) containing lots of different parts or ideas

coordinate (koh-**or**-duh-nate) to organize activities or people so that they all work together

craftworkers (**kraft**-wur-kurz) people skilled at making things with their hands

durable (**dur**-uh-buhl) tough and lasting for a long time

foreman (**for**-muhn) someone who leads a group of people who work together

mechanical (muh-**kan**-uh-kuhl) to do with machines or tools mortar (**mor**-tur) a mixture of lime, cement, sand, and water that is used for building

renovated (**ren**-uh-vate-id) having restored something to good condition, or made it more modern

scaffolds (**skaf**-uhldz) temporary platforms on which workers sit or stand as they work on a building

schedules (**skej**-oolz) plans, programs, or timetables

stamina (**stam**-uh-nuh) the energy and strength to keep doing something for a long time

structures (**struhk**-churz) things that have been built, such as a house, an office building, a bridge, or a dam

Aaseng, Nathan. *Building the Impossible.* Minneapolis, MN: Oliver Press, 1999.

Macaulay, David. *Building Big.* Boston, MA: Houghton Mifflin Company, 2000.

Morkes, Andrew (editor) *Ferguson's Career in Focus: Construction.* New York: Ferguson Publishing Company, 2001.

Pasternak, Ceel and Linda Thornburg. *Cool Careers for Girls in Construction.* Manassas Park, VA: Impact Publications, 2000.

Organizations

Building Construction Workers IU 330

c/o IDC Hall

616 East Burnside Street

Portland, OR 97214-1217

www.iww.org/iu330

National Association of Women in Construction

327 South Adams Street

Fort Worth, TX 76104

www.nawic.org

Web Site

Building Big

http://www.pbs.org/wgbh/buildingbig/index.html

This Web site is full of fascinating information, including the histories and explanations of how bridges, domes, skyscrapers, dams, and tunnels are built. You can even take the "challenges" yourself and build your own structures in an interactive game section. Biographies of ten famous engineers and architects are also included.

About the Author

Rachel O'Connor is a children's book editor living and working in New York City. She holds a B.A. in, English and French from University College Dublin in Ireland. The world of construction is of particular interest to Rachel—her grandfather owned his own construction company in Ireland.